Tincture of the Heart

Cecilia Tarvena Brizuela

BookLeaf Publishing

Presentation by *BookLeaf Publishing*

Web: www.bookleafpub.com

E-mail: info@bookleafpub.com

ISBN: 978-93-5774-659-5

First edition 2023

Will you miss me when I'm gone?

Will you miss me when I'm gone
When the kids are all grown and they have their
own adventures
Will you miss when I'm gone
Will you just think of me just lying down on the
sofa dreaming
Will you miss me when I'm gone
Will you miss me when you finally have your
dream come true?
Will you miss me when I'm gone
When all the sparkles surround you?
Will you miss me when I'm gone
And when all the struggles eases down and you
are finally comfortable?
Will you miss me when I'm gone and you wake
up to another place and time?
Will you miss me when I'm gone?

Borrowed Time

The life well planned twisted itself to its own
roller coaster ride
Casting light on the not listed chaos
of dusted pride
What can life be when efforts are in vain and it's
journey stole
The creeper of hopelessness came across that
vinyl emotions toils
What can life be when it is ceasing
rampant disarray
Have mercy to this fate!
A life going in dismay
This darkness I see I know need to end
For the clock ticks and I need to mend
Life's struggles are not life at all
It's a test of faith because fate is nothing but a
call
To fight for the kind of love you choose to
embrace
Kneading through a map written to efface
Oh God of mercy, extend my life and make me
cancer free
So I can have time to prepare the lives you
gifted me.

Death

Bid not to sneak on me.
I have to hug one last time,
Kiss one more time.

Seek not for God has a plan
For me to walk an unthreaded path
of legacy and love.

Look the other way for now,
And when the time comes
Let calm envelope me.

Let angels sing not only for my soul
But for the people I leave behind
That they remember me by the warmth of the
sun.

That the breeze lingers as a kiss.
Flowers bloom and a reminder of a laughter
unceasing and gay lifting spirits up!

Love

Plenitude calls
into the wildest timing in life
Searching deliberately for deliverance
Array of expectations melts solitude
Beloved dancing out of tune

Rays of sunshine as snow falls
enveloping roses embracing then withers with
cold
Sighing on that promise of joy
Seeking just fortune to hold

Flicker of lights gives indignant solace
to satiric union in default
Giving rise to happy disposition unknowingly
witnessing sparks of magic longing for happy
endings to stories untold!

Living

Skimming through the vastness
of life's tales and sorts
Lives a tangled stories of joyous
Journey and adventures
Climbing mountains, sliding on slopes
Driving and jumping on hoops
Unplanned trips, frolics on plains
Had the best memories of all

Embrace each day and laugh through pain
Life is long dying is short
Be still when tested, love not scorn
Thread through lanes, jump on puddles
Stare at the moon and wink at the stars
Test your limits, have your toes in the sand
It is the joy on getting lost that you are found

Grateful

As the sun rises I lift my heart with hopes and
dreams for my little ones
As the sun rises I raise my spirit up for healing
and love
As the sun rises I raise my gratefulness to the
universe
As the sun rises I celebrate the glory of the one
who created it
As the sun rises I free my emotions of hate and
worldly things
As the sun rises I am celebrating that I am still
here.

Hope

Digging through, disguised in sadness
Embellished in remorse of a past that stays
Not wanting to let go, fielding on torn
soul coiled, dormant.

In pitch black yielding memories
Flooding in rushed, surprised but warm
Caught in emotion poignant happy and peaceful.

Unrecognized but felt hope
Witnessed in silence coned in its own turmoil
Waiting to be unleashed on its own splendour
unscathed!

More to come, be settled
There might be no other that could match to
what stillness could offer
Be settled ... peace will come.

On love and life

Redefining life
Redesigning success
Re-examining goals
To include living meaningfully

Strengthening connections
Relearning communications
Establishing relationships
To love better and make memories

Smiling often
Sleeping better
Sending gratitude
For happiness not fleeting

For time gone is forever
Life lost is wasted chances
Love not shared is not love at all
And life without it is no life at all

Visions and Dreams

Softer views of the world
Harder ideas to fulfill
Strong ideals to prosper
Limitless ideologies that lingers

Stepping into the world of unknown
Takes knowing the basics as foundation to be
known
Tasking but uplifting courage leaves
Definite mark on this world

Testing the path with trodden meaning
Creates velocity attracting possibilities
Embracing potential takes energy
Unbeknownst to the world but you!

Dogma

Dance to quiet the heart
Sing to still the thoughts
Sleep to awaken the spirit
Stand up for the truth to conquer ignorance

Specific roles, unspecified journeys
Unraveled truth, amplified realities
Vigilant mind sifts through characters
Strong personalities not always bequest courage

Darkness relinquished by light
Knowing does not make perfection
Stillness does not mean inaction
Longing taken to higher levels conspires
accomplishments

Journey

It is by chance I get to see the world
It is by looking that I've unseen realities
It is by being still that I begin to dance
It is by loving that I understood courage

Courage it is that made me take the chance
A chance to let go of the past
The past that tied me to unclear realities
Realities that drove me to fantasy.

Life became easy when it bids it is ending
Ending does not at all mean dying
Dying does not mean saying goodbye
But the beginning of eternal peace.

Existence

Throngs of people
People alone in their own world
World that redefined every bit of existence
Changing what is external to innermost desire
Desire for worldly things
Things that clutters
Clutters that creates noise
Noise that clouds peace
Letting go to quiet down the spirit
Spirit that will expand horizons
Horizons that brightens peoples mind
Mind that allows simple joys
We have a choice to chase experiences
Experiences that puts meaning to relationships
Relationships that nurtures love and affectation
Affections that nourish healthy emotions
For life is too short to be attached to worldly
things
Things that does not matter when we go to the
final goodbye to worldly things
They are just things.

Promise

Pressed for time that's how it feels
Doubling the tasks that energy can deal
Tackling the enormous journey ahead
Facing the world fast paced
Too many things to accomplish unfazed
Daunting it is to move forward
But courage we abide to continue
Littered mind shall not prevail
Life's precious command is to sail
To live and love it entails
To hold on and embrace possibilities
Take the oar reach the shore
And embrace whatever unfolds
The positivity beholds a future
Foretold not but God knows you've been told

Sisters

Rummaging through the highlights of life
And looking at old photographs
The love and bond with my sisters are the
strongest one
Lots of love, including the tough kind
And we are now in a place and time
That memories built powers dreams and had an
attachment to mankind!
What we are we did not cause alone, who we are
we are not solely responsible
Our parents did endowed us with a lavish gift
that cannot be sold
We all have a future full of adventures
Attaching to things is just mere lure
Now I am praying for more time so the
things we talk about as a child we can explore
To touch the clouds and roam
For we have built a fort that is now strong
And we indeed made a castle of our own.

Story time

Sailors and dreamers were forced to a boat
Joined by throngs of incapacitated beasts from a
forest where trees plays a flute
And so they would jump and holler and who
knows what else they did
The sailors and dreamers were captivated by it
After a long confused days and nights observing
the feat
The sailors' hearts starts to thump and behold
there were fifteen of them dancing to unheard
beat
The dreamers were quiet and would nod at times
but announced loudly, not interested, we are
fine!
Day and night this life went on, until one sailor
fell with a sigh!
The dreamers observed and became callous, and
would just stare and glare
And they would sit and flick their hands with
flair
They ponder, and wonder why this is fair
To be put in a boat with no planned fare
And a boy they did not know about, this boat is
his lair

These throng of men didn't know he exist, but
for the boy happy in his mind this is no mare!
He began to write and sketch and made
characters out of them, and these wonderful days
he saw was a time with plan to spare
At last the boat reached the shore and the beasts
scampers
The sailors thought what fun without having to
plan
Just jump up and down and say it's all done
While the dreamers were forlorn
What a waste, what a waste they shook their
heads and say... I left my pen, I left my pad
I could have written a book while experiencing
this useless fad.
The boy never heard any of these, he held his
new book and ran out of pad
So he took his shirt off, and wrote on it fast
The ending of a life unexpectedly marvelous a
life he have had!

Proposal

Token taken and embellished with gold
Taken to a place and forgotten old
Skipped hopped and plastered few
Until broken and wanted kindled new.

Time gone and waiting had grown past
Deadline met with uncertainty
Nibbled truth will never be found true
For what is left may have to be started anew

Happy thoughts forced to grow
Now sown to heart it flows
No need to walk the altar to bless this duo
For love passed the test and genuinely due

Resolutions

Palladium of emotions thats shields
From the vastness of the world
Shine through and take the step to tackle the
impossible
The life you lead is the joy'll have.

Nurture your inner voice to speak loudly when
needed
So the vast majority of your senses awaken to
the tale of success
Unfolding daily for you to behold imprinting a
legacy.

Life as it is, does not end
It continues to the generations that had the
chance to behold the ignorance quashed
By commanding courage and dominance to a
chance that is once a dream!

Miracle

Futile may seem to tread through fear
Masking the ideas of defeat
Chances taken by the lure of courage
Strikes through hope and love it seems
Death was once feared
Now masters life instead
To stand against the scarcity of joy
Mountain of faith brought throngs of miracles
Unfolding as life ensues
To change the history and establish a home
Not taken for granted but made stronger by
hope!

Family

Bowing to a resigned life
Of love and compassion
To till the land of passion
Unbounded and secure!
Love wowed by life
Challenges by circumstance
Destiny withheld
Fighting for a chance
To grow more and behold
The magic of life
As it unfolds to teach
A life lived by sacrifice
Centered through faith
And love!

Nanay (Mother)

You understood my heart before I could make a
sound
You wiped my tears before it falls
You had me loved before I was born
You cuddled me close before I hurt a ton
You're a gift that keeps on giving
You modeled the love a mother should have
The life you lead will grow
In the hearts of your children
And the children thereof
What an honor what a chance
To mirror your life
Thank you for this love I'll not keep alone
But will shower others so you'll know
That your love will forever aglow!

Tatay (Father)

Daughters all four you have
Raised to rule with a heart
With dreams infused
And wisdom to tell
You held our hands and taught us to spell
You spread the books in front of us
Before we can even tell letters apart
You put music to your own words
To sing us bedtime lullaby
Your wisdom is not for telling alone
You lived those words and showed us the ropes
To live a life not attached to things but a life of
adventure and experience it brings
And I must say and not forget
That your care for us is such a joy
We grew and watched you model a love to the
woman you truly love!